# TYRANNOSAURUS

## and Other Dinosaurs of North America

by Dougal Dixon

illustrated by
Steve Weston and James Field

PICTURE WINDOW BOOKS
Minneapolis, Minnesota

Picture Window Books
5115 Excelsior Boulevard
Suite 232
Minneapolis, MN 55416
877-845-8392
www.picturewindowbooks.com

Printed in the United States of America.

**Library of Congress Cataloging-in-Publication Data**
Dixon, Dougal.
Tyrannosaurus and other dinosaurs of North America
/ by Dougal Dixon ; illustrated by Steve Weston &
James Field.
p. cm. – (Dinosaur find)
Includes bibliographical references and index.
ISBN-13: 978-1-4048-2265-8 (library binding)
ISBN-10: 1-4048-2265-8 (library binding)
ISBN-13: 978-1-4048-2271-9 (paperback)
ISBN-10: 1-4048-2271-2 (paperback)
1. Dinosaurs–North America–Juvenile literature.
I. Weston, Steve, ill. II. Field, James, 1959- ill. III. Title.
QE861.5.D674 2007
567.9097–dc22                    2006027944

**Acknowledgments**
This book was produced for Picture Window Books by
Bender Richardson White, U.K.

Illustrations by James Field (pages 4–5, 7, 11, 15, 19)
and Steve Weston (cover and pages 1, 9, 13, 17, 21).
Diagrams by Stefan Chabluk.

Photographs: Corbis page 18. Digital Vision page 14.
Getty Images pages 10, 12, 20. istockphotos pages 6
(Michael Chen), 8 (Sebastien Burel), 16 (Melody
Kerchhoff).

Consultant: John Stidworthy, Scientific Fellow of
the Zoological Society, London, and former
Lecturer in the Education Department, Natural History
Museum, London.

Reading Adviser: Susan Kesselring, M.A., Literacy
Educator, Rosemount–Apple Valley–Eagan
(Minnesota) School District

## Types of dinosaurs

In this book, a red shape at the
top of a left-hand page shows
the animal was a meat-eater.
A green shape shows it was
a plant-eater.

## Just how big—or small—
## were they?

Dinosaurs were many different
sizes. We have compared their
size to one of the following:

Chicken
2 feet (60 centimeters) tall
Weight 6 pounds (2.7 kilograms)

Adult person
6 feet (1.8 meters) tall
Weight 170 pounds (76.5 kg)

Elephant
10 feet (3 m) tall
Weight 12,000 pounds
(5,400 kg)

# Table of Contents

# What's Inside?

Dinosaurs! These dinosaurs lived in places that now form North America. Find out how they survived millions of years ago and what they have in common with today's animals.

# LIFE IN NORTH AMERICA

Dinosaurs lived between 230 million and 65 million years ago. The world did not look the same then. The land and seas were not in the same places as today. Many kinds of dinosaurs lived on the land that became North America.

On the edge of a forest, a spiky *Gastonia* used its armor to keep away a fierce *Acrocanthosaurus*. Ahead of them, two *Falcarius* looked on, ready to run out of the way.

# FALCARIUS

*Falcarius* belonged to the group of dinosaurs that were meat-eaters. But unlike its relatives, *Falcarius* ate mostly plants. It used long, curved claws to rip up plants and pull down branches to eat. Feathers covered this dinosaur and kept it warm.

### Plant-eating meat-eater today

The modern panda belongs to a meat-eating group of mammals, but like *Falcarius*, it eats mostly plants. Bamboo plants are the panda's favorite food.

Size Comparison

With strong front legs,
*Falcarius* pulled
down a tree branch.
Then it used clawed
fingers to pull off
leaves and twigs
to eat.

7

# SUUWASSEA

*Suuwassea* was a long-necked plant-eater. At 40 feet (12 meters) long, this dinosaur was big, but it lived among relatives that were even bigger. *Suuwassea* moved, fed, and slept in herds. It was always on the lookout for predators seeking an easy kill.

## Many species today

Herds of modern plant-eaters like zebra and wildebeest gather at water holes. They come to feed and drink, like *Suuwassea* did long ago.

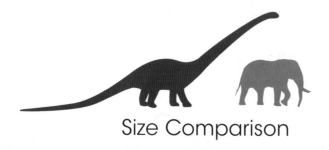

Size Comparison

A hungry *Tyrannosaurus* snapped at flying reptiles called *Pterosaurs* as they came near. *Tyrannosaurus* and the reptiles were looking for prey, dead or alive.

13

# STEGOSAURUS

Pronunciation:
STEG-o-SAW-rus

*Stegosaurus* was a plant-eating dinosaur. It had plates down its back and tail and spikes on the end of its tail. The plates protected the *Stegosaurus* from attacks by predators. By swinging its tail, a *Stegosaurus* could use the spikes as weapons.

### Show-offs today

An African elephant sticks out its ears to make itself look bigger and more threatening, much like the way a *Stegosaurus* used its plates to look bigger.

Size Comparison

When under attack, the *Stegosaurus* probably turned sideways so its plates and spikes would frighten the attacker.

# BAROSAURUS

*Barosaurus* was a plant-eater with a particularly long neck. Its body was lightweight, so it could rise on its hind legs to feed on treetops. *Barosaurus* used peg-like teeth to strip leaves from twigs.

## A long neck today

Today, the giraffe has the longest neck of any animal. But unlike the *Barosaurus*, it cannot rise on its hind legs.

Size Comparison

A group of *Barosaurus* lifted up their small heads to feed on treetops. *Barosaurus* reached to the height of a four-story building.

*Gastonia* was heavily armored. It was covered in spikes and plates. It needed to be. All kinds of fierce meat-eaters wanted to eat *Gastonia*. When attacked, it crouched low to protect its soft underbelly.

### Defensive animals today

Modern African buffalo use their horns to defend against predators, much like *Gastonia* once used its spikes.

Size Comparison

A *Gastonia* prepared to defend against a group of *Utahraptor*. *Gastonia* used its spikes for protection, not as weapons.

# MONTANOCERATOPS

Pronunciation:
mon-TAN-uh-SER-uh-tops

*Montanoceratops* was a small, horned dinosaur. The horns were only tiny knobs on its nose, not giant structures like those of its relative, *Triceratops*. *Montanoceratops* had a frill around its neck and a beak for nipping off the shoots of plants.

## Colored signals today

The saddlebill stork uses the bright colors on its head as signals, like *Montanoceratops* did long ago.

Size Comparison

Little *Montanoceratops* often looked for food alongside the big horned dinosaur *Triceratops*. *Montanoceratops* used the brightly colored patches on its frill to signal to mates.

# Where Did They Go?

Dinosaurs are extinct, which means that none of them are alive today. Scientists study rocks and fossils to find clues about what happened to dinosaurs.

People have different explanations about what happened. Some people think a huge asteroid hit Earth and caused all sorts of climate changes, which caused the dinosaurs to die. Others think volcanic eruptions caused the climate to change and that killed the dinosaurs. No one knows for sure what happened to all of the dinosaurs.

# Glossary

**armor**—protective covering of plates, horns, spikes, or clubs used for fighting

**beak**—the hard front part of the mouth of birds and some dinosaurs; also called a bill

**claws**—tough, usually curved fingernails or toenails

**herd**—large group of animals that move, feed, and sleep together

**mammals**—warm-blooded animals that have hair and drink mother's milk when they are young

**plate**—a large, flat, usually tough structure on the body

**prey**—animals that are hunted by other animals for food; the hunters are known as predators

**sail**—a thin, upright structure on the back of some animals

**scavenger**—a meat-eater that feeds on animals that are already dead

**signal**—to make a sign, warning, or hint

# TO LEARN MORE

## AT THE LIBRARY

Clark, Neil, and William Lindsay. *1001 Facts About Dinosaurs.* New York: Backpack Books, Dorling Kindersley, 2002.

Dixon, Dougal. *Dougal Dixon's Amazing Dinosaurs.* Honesdale, Pa.: Boyds Mills Press, 2000.

Holtz, Thomas, and Michael Brett-Surman. *Dinosaur Field Guide.* New York: Random House, 2001.

## ON THE WEB

FactHound offers a safe, fun way to find Web sites related to this book. All of the sites on FactHound have been researched by our staff.

1. Visit *www.facthound.com*
2. Type in this special code: 1404822658
3. Click on the FETCH IT button.

Your trusty FactHound will fetch the best Web sites for you!

# INDEX

## LOOK FOR ALL OF THE BOOKS IN THE DINOSAUR FIND SERIES: